Life Stories
Nelson Mandela

Richard Killeen

Illustrated by David McAllister

WAYLAND

Life Stories

Louis Braille

Christopher Columbus

Grace Darling

Guy Fawkes

Anne Frank

Gandhi

Helen Keller

Martin Luther King

Nelson Mandela

Florence Nightingale

Shakespeare

Mother Teresa

Cover and title page: Nelson Mandela in London in 1990,
the year of his release from prison.

Editor: Polly Goodman
Designer: Joyce Chester

First published in 1995 by
Wayland (Publishers) Ltd
61 Western Road, Hove
East Sussex BN3 1JD, England

British Library Cataloguing in Publication Data
Killeen, Richard
Nelson Mandela. – (Life Stories)
I. Title II. McAllister, David
III. Series
322.44092

ISBN 0 7502 1616 6

Typeset by Joyce Chester, England
Printed and bound in Italy by G. Canale and C.S.p.A., Turin

Contents

Words in **bold** are explained in the glossary on page 30.

The young Nelson

Nelson Mandela was born on 18 July 1918. He was the son of a royal chief in Transkei, a part of South Africa. When he was only nine years old, Nelson's father died. He was sent to live with the head chief of his people, the Thembu. This man adopted Nelson as his own son.

▼ Nelson in the village where he grew up.

▲ Nelson lived in this hut when he was a boy.

Nelson was brought up in the traditional way of the Thembu people. He learned old customs which had been passed on from parents to children for hundreds of years. But he also got a good modern education. When Nelson was sixteen he was sent to boarding school. Then when he was twenty-one he went to Fort Hare University to study for a degree.

However, Nelson did not finish his degree at Fort Hare. He left in his third year and headed to the great city of Johannesburg. There were gold mines and diamond mines near the city which had made South Africa rich. But the white people kept all the wealth and power for themselves. White people ran South Africa, yet most of the people in the country were black and had almost nothing.

▲ Johannesburg is the biggest and richest city in South Africa.

Nelson soon met an estate agent called Walter Sisulu, who got him a job in a law firm. This gave Nelson enough money to continue his degree, which he finished in 1942. After this, Nelson decided to become a **lawyer**, so he began to study law at the University of Witswatersrand in Johannesburg. Nelson continued to work at the law firm while studying.

In 1945, Nelson married his first wife Evelyn. Their first child was born in 1946. He was called Thembi.

◀ Nelson met Walter Sisulu in Johannesburg.

The ANC and apartheid

Nelson's best friend at university was Oliver Tambo, who was another black law student. In 1944, Nelson and Oliver helped to start a group called the Youth League. This was part of an older organization called the **African National Congress (ANC),** which was working to get better treatment for black people in South Africa. By 1949, Nelson and the Youth League had taken control of the ANC.

▼ Nelson and Oliver Tambo help plan the Youth League.

▲ Nelson in the office of his law practice.

However by then, life for blacks in South Africa had got worse because the **government** wanted to separate black people and white people completely. Its word for this was **apartheid** (pronounced 'a–par–tide').

Meanwhile, Nelson's law studies were going badly because he was spending so much time working for the ANC. But he eventually became a lawyer in 1951. A year later, Nelson and Oliver Tambo set up the first-ever black law practice in Johannesburg. By now, Nelson and Evelyn had a second son.

Apartheid made life very hard for black people in South Africa. ▶

Nelson and the other ANC leaders hated apartheid because it meant that blacks could not live in certain areas, could not vote, and could not use the same services as white people. So they organized **strikes**, **boycotts** and other **protests**. They broke apartheid laws and held noisy public meetings all over the country. The police often attacked them and there was a lot of violence. In 1952, Nelson was put in charge of these public protests for all of South Africa. He also became head of the ANC in Transvaal, the rich area which included Johannesburg.

◀ An apartheid sign at the beach. Black people were not allowed on this beach.

Then the government arrested Nelson because he was a danger to its rule. It used one of the worst apartheid laws against him and **'banned'** him. This meant that Nelson could not attend any public meetings, could only meet one person at a time, and was watched closely by the police the whole time. Nelson was a prisoner in his own home.

▼ A protest against apartheid.

Fighting for freedom

Three years later, in 1955, Nelson went to a big **rally** near Johannesburg. It was a very important rally because it was held by the Congress Alliance. This was a new organization which was the first group to include both black people and white people. Nelson went to the rally in disguise because he was still banned by the government and was not allowed to go.

▼ The Congress Alliance rally. Nelson wore the blue uniform of a driver so that the police would not recognize him.

The Congress Alliance scared the government because it was more dangerous to its rule than the ANC. So Nelson was arrested again at the rally, along with 155 others. They were all put on a trial which dragged on for four and a half years. This trial was called the Treason Trial.

▲ A special bus took Nelson (right) and the others to the Treason Trial.

Nelson and
Winnie on their
wedding day.

In between visits to the court for the Treason Trial, Nelson carried on his work for the ANC.

In 1956 Nelson's marriage to Evelyn ended in divorce. Soon afterwards, he met and fell in love with a young social worker called Winnie Madikizela. Winnie and Nelson were married in 1958. Nelson had to get special permission from the government to get married because he was still banned!

In 1960, Nelson led huge protests after the Sharpeville **massacre**. This was when police killed sixty-nine demonstrators and wounded over 200 others at the town of Sharpeville, near Johannesburg. It was the worst crime of the apartheid government. Nelson was arrested once more at the protests, along with most of the other ANC leaders. Only Oliver Tambo escaped and fled abroad.

The Sharpeville massacre was in newspapers all over the world. ▶

Nelson led angry protests after the massacre. ▼

Nelson was not held for long however. The Treason Trials finally collapsed in 1961 and he was released and 'un-banned' for the first time in years. However, Nelson knew that the government would try to arrest him again if it could, so he went into hiding. Even though Nelson went everywhere secretly, he soon became one of the most famous names in South Africa.

▲ This was the last photograph of Nelson before he went to prison.

Then Nelson went to other African countries to get help and money for the ANC. He was not supposed to go out of the country and he had no **passport** to travel. But Nelson went anyway, knowing that he would be arrested on his return. He was right. On 5 August 1962, the police caught him near Durban. Nelson spent the next twenty-eight years in jail.

Long years in jail

On 7 November 1962, Nelson was found guilty of leaving South Africa without a passport. He was sent to jail for five years. First he went to a prison in Pretoria, then to Robben Island.

▼ The judge passes sentence on Nelson.

Robben Island Prison can be seen from the beaches near Cape Town. No one has ever escaped from it to this day. Nelson was not long there when he was brought back to Pretoria to be accused of leading the ANC's army. He was found guilty again and might have been hanged, but the judge sent him back to Robben Island – this time for life. Nelson was forty-six years old.

Back at Robben Island, Nelson was put in a tiny cell where he was kept for sixteen hours each day. He was allowed very little contact with Winnie and his family. He could only write and receive one letter every six months.

Nelson in his cell. ▶

▼ Prisoners at work in the yard of Robben Island prison.

Every day, Nelson had to get up at 5 am. By 7 am, he was at work. This meant breaking stones, or gathering seaweed on the shore, or working with a pickaxe in a stone quarry. At noon, lunch came in a big drum for the prisoners to eat. It was poor food and tasted bad. Then there was more work until the middle of the afternoon.

By 4 pm Nelson was back in his cell. He was supposed to be in bed by 8 pm, but as the years went by, he was sometimes allowed to stay up late to read, which he loved. Nelson spent nearly twenty years like this on Robben Island, over 7,000 days and 7,000 nights. Every day was the same.

▲ Nelson's tiny cell on Robben Island.

▼ Nelson breaking stones in the prison quarry.

21

Nelson stayed on Robben Island until 1982, when he was moved to Pollsmoor Prison near Cape Town. By now Nelson was the most famous prisoner in the world.

Nelson was in prison with his friend Walter Sisulu. Here they are talking in the prison yard.

At the same time, other countries were changing their opinion about South Africa. Its government was unpopular all over the world because of apartheid. In South Africa the black **townships** were rising up in anger. The words on everyone's lips were: 'Free Nelson Mandela.'

A new government, under **President** F.W. de Klerk, decided that the only way to solve South Africa's problems was to release Nelson from prison.

▼ Students all over the world wanted Nelson freed from prison.

Release and triumph

On Sunday 11 February 1990, Nelson Mandela walked free at last. He and Winnie walked together through the prison gates while millions of people all around the world watched them on television. Nelson was now seventy-one years old, but he looked much younger.

▲ Free at last, Nelson gives the victory salute.

Later that day, Nelson spoke to a huge crowd in Cape Town. He told them that the fight for equal rights would continue. And so it did. Nelson began to talk to President de Klerk and his ministers about a new system of government for South Africa, one which would be fair to everybody.

Nelson and Winnie in front of the prison gates. ▼

Meanwhile, Nelson had become one of the most famous people in the world. Now that he was free, everyone wanted to meet him. He visited the USA, Britain, France and many other countries, and even met the Pope. In Sweden, Nelson met his old friend and partner Oliver Tambo, who had been his best friend at university over fifty years earlier.

Nelson and ▶ President de Klerk worked together to make South Africa a better country.

▲ Huge crowds greeted Nelson when he went back to Soweto after his release.

The ANC was made legal once more and the unfair apartheid system was removed. Nelson and President de Klerk slowly moved South Africa towards a **democratic** government.

Nelson and Oliver Tambo meet for the first time in thirty years. ▼

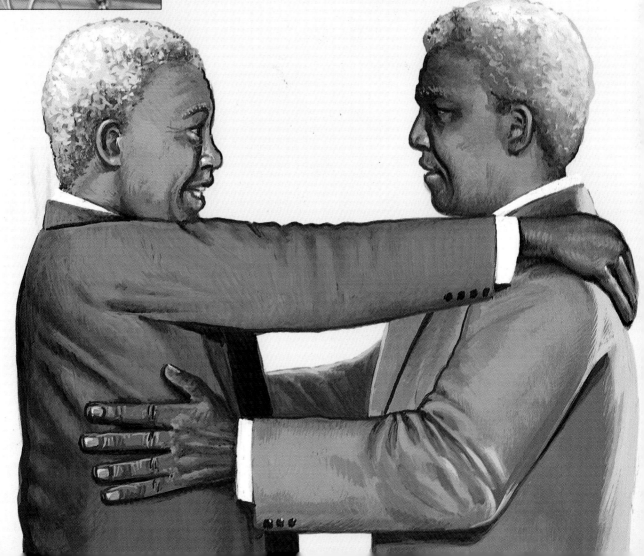

▼ Nelson makes a speech before the elections of 1994.

However, there were many problems. Many white people, including President de Klerk, did not want full democracy. And there were many black people who were against the ANC. For example, the **Zulu** people feared that their special way of life would disappear if black and white people mixed together in a **multi-racial** South Africa.

▲ President Mandela takes the oath to be his country's leader.

But in the end, Nelson and President de Klerk got over most of the problems and together they won the 1993 Nobel Peace Prize.

In April 1994, the first free, democratic **elections** in South African history made Nelson Mandela president of his country. Nelson's long struggle for freedom had ended in triumph. The man who spent twenty-eight years in apartheid jails is now president of a new South Africa.

Glossary

African National Congress (ANC) The group who have worked to get the same rights for black people as white people in South Africa.

apartheid The system that completely separated black people from white people.

banned Under the system of apartheid, not allowed to attend public meetings, meet more than one person at a time or talk to another banned person.

boycotts Refusals to buy certain goods or use certain services. Boycotts can be used to make the people who make goods or provide services lose money.

democratic Where there are equal rights for all the people in a country. In a democracy, every adult man and woman can say who they want to be their leader.

elections The choosing of the leaders of a country.

government The group of people who rule a country.

lawyer A person who is an expert in the law.

massacre The violent killing of a large number of people.

multi-racial Including many races.

passport A document that gives permission to travel abroad.

president The leader of a country which is a republic.

protest To object strongly.

rally A gathering together of people in order to protest against something.

strikes Stopping work until certain demands have been met.

townships Under apartheid, poor areas where blacks were forced to live.

Zulu One of the principal black peoples in South Africa, mainly found in Natal and the Eastern Cape.

Date chart

1918 Nelson Mandela is born in Transkei on 18 July.
1934 Becomes a boarder in Healdtown High School.
1939 Enters Fort Hare University College, in Ciskei.
1941 Goes to Johannesburg and works in a law office.
1942 Starts to study law at Witswatersrand University.
1944 Co-founder of the Youth League of the ANC.
1945 Marries Evelyn Ntoko Mase.
1946 Birth of Nelson and Evelyn's first child, Thembi.
1948 National Party government establishes system of apartheid.
1949 Youth League takes over the ANC.

1951 Qualifies as a lawyer.
1952 Founds the first black law partnership with Oliver Tambo.
Banned by the government under apartheid laws.
1955 Founder member of the Congress Alliance.
1956 One of the defendants in the Treason Trial.
1958 Second marriage, to Winnie Madikizela.
1960 Sharpeville massacre.
1962 Arrested for leaving South Africa without a passport. Spends next twenty-eight years in jail.
1990 Released from prison on 11 February.
1994 Elected President of South Africa on 27 April.

Books to read

Long Walk to Freedom by Nelson Mandela, (Little Brown, 1994)
Mandela for Beginners by Tony Pinchuck, (Icon Books, 1994)
South Africa: A Modern History, by T.R.H. Davenport, 4th edition (Macmillan, 1991)

Index

The publishers would like to thank the
following for allowing their photographs to be
used in this book: Associated Press (Peter
Magubane) 13; Camera Press 16 (Eli Weinberg),
26 (Jan Kopec), 27 (Tiddy Maitland-Titterton);
Eye Ubiquitous 6–7; John Frost Historical
Newspapers 15; Impact Photos *Cover*, Title page
(John Arthur), 10 (E. Andrews), 25 (John
Arthur), 29 (Carolina Salguero); Mayibuye
Centre 4–5, 9 (top), 14, 18, 20, 22; Topham
Picture Source 9 (bottom).